GREAT WORDS OF JESUS

LION PUBLISHING

Good news for the poor

On the Sabbath Jesus went as usual
to the synagogue. He stood up to
read the Scriptures and was handed
the book of the prophet Isaiah. He
unrolled the scroll and found the
place where it is written,
'The Spirit of the Lord is upon me,
because he has chosen me to bring
good news to the poor.
He has sent me to proclaim liberty to
the captives
and recovery of sight to the blind;
to set free the oppressed
and announce that the time has come
when the Lord will save his people.'

Jesus rolled up the scroll, gave it back
to the attendant, and sat down. All
the people in the synagogue had
their eyes fixed on him, as he said to
them, 'This passage of scripture has
come true today, as you heard it
being read.'

Luke 4:16-21

For peasant farmers, poverty is a factor of life

Take my yoke

'Come to me', Jesus said, 'all of you
who are tired from carrying heavy
loads, and I will give you rest. Take

my yoke and put it on you, and learn from me, because I am gentle and humble in spirit; and you will find rest. For the yoke I will give you is easy, and the load I will put on you is light.'

Matthew 11:28-30

Hear me

Anyone who comes to me and listens to my words and obeys them – I will show you what he is like. He is like a man who, in building his house, dug deep and laid the foundation on rock. The river overflowed and hit that house but could not shake it, because it was well built. But anyone

who hears my words and does not
obey them is like a man who built his
house without laying a foundation;
when the flood hit that house it fell
at once – and what a terrible crash
that was!

Luke 6:47-49

Conversation piece beneath the walls of Jerusalem

Finding life

'If anyone wants to come with me,'
Jesus said,'he must forget self, carry
his cross, and follow me. For
whoever wants to save his own life
will lose it; but whoever loses his life
for me and for the gospel will save it.
Does a person gain anything if he
wins the whole world but loses his
life? Of course not! There is nothing
he can give to regain his life.'

Mark 8:34-37

Giant poppies reach towards the sun

The bread of life

Jesus said . . . 'It is my Father who gives you the real bread from heaven. For the bread that God gives is he who comes down from heaven and gives life to the world.'

'Sir,' they asked him, 'give us this bread always.'

'I am the bread of life,' Jesus told them. 'He who comes to me will never be hungry; he who believes in me will never be thirsty . . .

'I will never turn away anyone who comes to me.'

John 6:32-35, 37

Flat loaves of bread

The light of the world

'I am the light of the world,' Jesus said. 'Whoever follows me will have the light of life and will never walk in darkness.'

John 8:12

Dawn in the Dardanelles

The gate for the sheep

Jesus said again, 'I am telling you the truth: I am the gate for the sheep. All others who came before me are thieves and robbers, but the sheep did not listen to them.

'I am the gate. Whoever comes in by me will be saved; he will come in and go out and find pasture. The thief comes only in order to steal, kill, and destroy. I have come in order that you might have life – life in all its fullness.'

John 10:7-10

The shepherd's flock seek out the shade on the terraced hillsides of Israel

The way

On the evening before his death,
Jesus said to his disciples: 'I am going
to prepare a place for you. I would
not tell you this if it were not so.
And after I go and prepare a place
for you, I will come back and take
you to myself, so that you will be
where I am. You know the way that
leads to the place where I am going.'

Thomas said to him, 'Lord, we do
not know where you are going; so
how can we know the way to get
there?'

Jesus answered him, 'I am the way,
the truth, and the life; no one goes to
the Father except by me.'

John 14:2-6

Stone steps mark the way in Israel

The good shepherd

I am the good shepherd, who is willing to die for the sheep. When the hired man, who is not a shepherd and does not own the sheep, sees a wolf coming, he leaves the sheep and runs away; so the wolf snatches the sheep and scatters them. The hired man runs away because he is only a hired man and does not care about the sheep.

I am the good shepherd. As the Father knows me and I know the Father, in the same way I know my sheep and they know me. And I am willing to die for them.

John 10:11-15

A shepherd with his flock amongst the olive trees in Israel

The vine

Jesus said: 'I am the real vine, and my Father is the gardener. He breaks off every branch in me that does not bear fruit, and he prunes every branch that does bear fruit, so that it will be clean and bear more fruit. You have been made clean already by the teaching I have given you. Remain united to me, and I will remain united to you. A branch cannot bear fruit by itself; it can do so only if it remains in the vine. In the same way you cannot bear fruit unless you remain in me.'

John 15:1-4

Branches are pruned to improve the yield of the vine

The resurrection and the life

Martha said to Jesus, 'If you had been here, Lord, my brother would not have died! But I know that even now God will give you whatever you ask him for.'

'Your brother will rise to life,' Jesus told her.

'I know,' she replied, 'that he will rise to life on the last day.'

Jesus said to her, 'I am the resurrection and the life. Whoever believes in me will live, even though he dies; and whoever lives and believes in me will never die. Do you believe this?'

John 11:21-26

The traditional site of Lazarus' tomb at Bethany

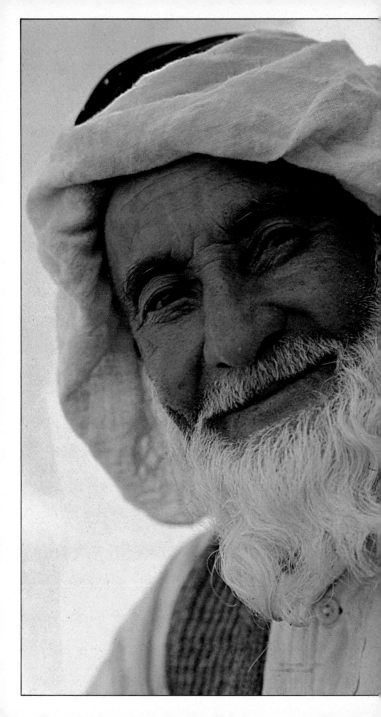

Hidden treasure

The Kingdom of heaven is like this. A man happens to find a treasure hidden in a field. He covers it up again, and is so happy that he goes and sells everything he has, and then goes back and buys that field.

Also, the Kingdom of heaven is like this. A man is looking for fine pearls, and when he finds one that is unusually fine, he goes and sells everything he has, and buys that pearl.

Matthew 13:44-46

A new birth

A Jewish leader called Nicodemus
came to Jesus with questions:
'I am telling you the truth,' Jesus told
him, 'no one can see the Kingdom of
God unless he is born again.'
'How can a grown man be born
again?' Nicodemus asked. 'He
certainly cannot enter his mother's
womb and be born a second time!'
'I am telling you the truth,' replied
Jesus. 'No one can enter the
Kingdom of God unless he is born of
water and the Spirit. A person is
born physically of human parents,
but he is born spiritually of the
Spirit. Do not be surprised because I
tell you that you must all be born
again . . .

'As Moses lifted up the bronze snake
on a pole in the desert, in the same
way the Son of Man must be lifted
up, so that everyone who believes in
him may have eternal life. For God
loved the world so much that he
gave his only Son, so that everyone
who believes in him may not die but
have eternal life.'

John 3:3-7, 14-17

A sparkling stream in Galilee

The people of the Kingdom

Jesus' disciples gathered round him, and he began to teach them:
'Happy are those who know they are spiritually poor;
the Kingdom of heaven belongs to them!
'Happy are those who mourn;
God will comfort them!
'Happy are those who are humble;
they will receive what God has promised!
'Happy are those whose greatest desire is to do what God requires;
God will satisfy them fully!
'Happy are those who are merciful to others;
God will be merciful to them!
'Happy are the pure in heart;
they will see God!
'Happy are those who work for peace;
God will call them his children!'

Matthew 5:3-9

Jesus teaches his followers

Love
your enemies

You have heard that it was said,
'Love your friends, hate your
enemies.' But now I tell you: love
your enemies and pray for those who
persecute you, so that you may
become the sons of your Father in
heaven.

Matthew 5:43-45

Conversation in a street in Aleppo, Syria

Don't condemn – forgive

Do not judge others, and God will
not judge you;
do not condemn others, and God will
not condemn you;
forgive others, and God will forgive
you.
Give to others, and God will give to
you.
Indeed, you will receive a full
measure, a generous helping, poured
into your hands – all that you can
hold.
The measure you use for others is the
one that God will use for you.

Luke 6:37-38

*Goods are weighed and measured in the market at
Bethlehem*

Light for the world

'You are like light for the whole world,' Jesus said. 'A city built on a hill cannot be hidden. No one lights a lamp and puts it under a bowl; instead he puts it on the lampstand, where it gives light for everyone in the house.

'In the same way your light must shine before people, so that they will see the good things you do and praise your Father in heaven.'

Matthew 5:14-16

Oil-lamps modelled on those in use in Bible times burn with a steady flame

Riches in heaven

'Do not store up riches for yourselves here on earth,' Jesus said, 'where moths and rust destroy, and robbers break in and steal.

'Instead, store up riches for yourselves in heaven, where moths and rust cannot destroy, and robbers cannot break in and steal. For your heart will always be where your riches are.'

Matthew 6:19-21

Gold drinking-vessels from ancient Persia

A lesson in how to pray

One day Jesus was praying in a certain place. When he had finished, one of his disciples said to him, 'Lord, teach us to pray, just as John taught his disciples.'

Jesus said to them, 'When you pray, say this:
"Father:
May your holy name be honoured;
may your Kingdom come.
Give us day by day the food we need,
Forgive us our sins, for we forgive
everyone who does us wrong.
And do not bring us to hard testing." '

Luke 11:1-4

Ripe ears of wheat to be turned into bread for a hungry world

Searching and finding

'Ask, and you will receive,' Jesus said, 'seek, and you will find; knock, and the door will be opened to you. For everyone who asks will receive, and anyone who seeks will find, and the door will be opened to him who knocks.

'Would any of you who are fathers give your son a stone when he asks for bread?
Or would you give him a snake when he asks for a fish?
Bad as you are, you know how to give good things to your children.
How much more, then, will your Father in heaven give good things to those who ask him!'

Matthew 7:7-11

Doors to the quaint cone-shaped dwellings of Cappadocia (Turkey)

The choice

No one can be a slave of two masters; he will hate one and love the other; he will be loyal to one and despise the other. You cannot serve both God and money.

Matthew 6:24

Roman coins showing the heads of emperors Tiberius and Claudius, from New Testament times

Serving others

Jesus said: 'The men who are considered rulers of the heathen have power over them, the leaders have complete authority. This, however, is not the way it is among you. If one of you wants to be great, he must be the servant of the rest; and if one of you wants to be first, he must be the slave of all. For even the Son of Man did not come to be served; he came to serve and to give his life to redeem many people.'

Mark 10:42-45

From ancient times to the present day donkeys have been man's beasts of burden

Love your neighbour

A teacher of the Law asked Jesus,
'Which is the greatest commandment
in the Law?'

Jesus answered, ' "Love the Lord your God with all your heart, with all your soul, and with all your mind." This is the greatest and the most important commandment. The second most important commandment is like it: "Love your neighbour as you love yourself." '

Matthew 22:35-39

Women work together to gather in the harvest

Like children

The disciples came to Jesus, asking,
'Who is the greatest in the Kingdom
of heaven?'

So Jesus called a child, made him
stand in front of them, and said,
'I assure you that unless you change
and become like children, you will
never enter the Kingdom of heaven.
The greatest in the Kingdom of
heaven is the one who humbles
himself and becomes like this child.
And whoever welcomes in my name
one such child as this, welcomes me.'

Matthew 18:1-5

Two Bedouin children from Jordan

God will provide

It is God who clothes the
wild grass – grass that is here today
and gone tomorrow, burnt up in the
oven. Won't he be all the more sure
to clothe you? How little faith you
have!
So do not start worrying: 'Where will
my food come from? or my drink ? or
my clothes?' (These are the things the
pagans are always concerned about.)
Your Father in heaven knows that
you need all these things.

Instead, be concerned above
everything else with the Kingdom of
God and with what he requires of
you, and he will provide you with all
these other things.

So do not worry about tomorrow; it
will have enough worries of its own.
There is no need to add to the
troubles each day brings.

Matthew 6:30-34

Flowers of Galilee

The promise of freedom

Jesus said to those who believed in him, 'If you obey my teaching, you are really my disciples; you will know the truth, and the truth will set you free.'

'We are the descendants of Abraham,' they answered, 'and we have never been anybody's slaves. What do you mean, then, by saying, "You will be free"?'

Jesus said to them, 'I am telling you the truth: everyone who sins is a slave of sin. A slave does not belong to a family permanently, but a son belongs there for ever. If the Son sets you free, then you will be really free.'

John 8:31-36

Eternal life

I am telling you the truth: whoever hears my words and believes in him who sent me has eternal life. He will not be judged, but has already passed from death to life.

John 5:24-25

Welcome and reward

'Whoever welcomes you,' Jesus said to his disciples, 'welcomes me; and whoever welcomes me welcomes the one who sent me. Whoever welcomes God's messenger because he is God's messenger, will share in his reward. And whoever welcomes a good man because he is good, will share in his reward.

'You can be sure that whoever gives even a drink of cold water to one of the least of these my followers because he is my follower, 'will certainly receive a reward.'

Matthew 10:40-42

A boy on a donkey passes through the Lion Gate, Jerusalem

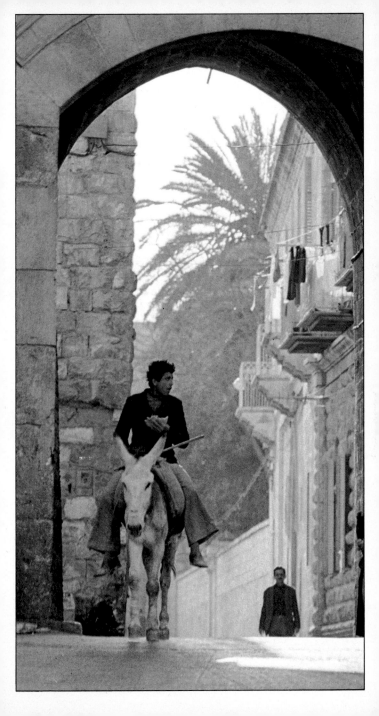

Answered prayer

Whenever two of you on earth agree about anything you pray for, it will be done for you by my Father in heaven.

For where two or three come together in my name, I am there with them.

Matthew 18:19-20

Last promises

When I go, you will not be left all alone; I will come back to you. In a little while the world will see me no more, but you will see me; and because I live, you also will live . . .

I have told you this while I am still with you. The Helper, the Holy Spirit, whom the Father will send in my name, will teach you everything and make you remember all that I have told you.

Peace is what I leave with you; it is my own peace that I give you. I do not give it as the world does. Do not be worried and upset; do not be afraid. You heard me say to you, 'I am leaving, but I will come back to you.'

John 14:18-19, 25-28

Boats on Lake Galilee

I will be with you always

After Jesus' death and resurrection: 'The eleven disciples went to the hill in Galilee where Jesus had told them to go. When they saw him, they worshipped him, even though some of them doubted.

Jesus drew near and said to them, 'I have been given all authority in heaven and on earth. Go, then, to all

peoples everywhere and make them my disciples: baptize them in the name of the Father, the Son, and the Holy Spirit, and teach them to obey everything I have commanded you. And I will be with you always, to the end of the age.'' '

Matthew 28:16-20

Sheep and shepherd on a coast road in Tunisia at sunset

ISBN 0 85648 158 0 (casebound edition)
    0 85648 182 3 (paperback edition)

Photographs by David Alexander: pages 1, 11,
21, 27, 33, 35, 37, 43; Peter Baker
Photographs: page 53 and endpapers; J. Allan
Cash: page 45; Fritz Fankhauser: pages 7,17,
19, 51, 55, 57, 59; Sonia Halliday
Photographs: F. H. C. Birch, pages 9, 24, 39,
Sonia Halliday, pages 5, 13, 41, 47, 63, Jane
Taylor, pages 29, 31, 49; Heather James: page
61; Middle East Photographic Archive: page
23; Rex Features: pages 3, 15

Quotations from *Good News Bible, Today's
English Version*, copyright 1966, 1971 and 1976
American Bible Society.

Printed in Great Britain